Ninja Creami Cookbook for Beginners

Healthy and Deliciously Simple Recipes for Mastering Your Ninja Creami

By

Isla S. Ashwood

Table of Contents

CHAPTER 7: MILKSHAKE

CONCLUSION

Introduction

Welcome to the amazing world of handmade frozen desserts with your Ninja Creami! Whether you're a seasoned ice cream aficionado or a curious beginner looking to discover the joys of making your own ice cream, sorbets, gelatos, and more, this cookbook is your ticket to a world of creamy, dreamy possibilities. The Ninja Creami stands out in the kitchen gadget landscape as a groundbreaking instrument that converts frozen ingredients into rich, creamy desserts with the press of a button. Its innovative technology enables unparalleled levels of customization and creativity, allowing you to create delicacies that are perfectly tailored to your taste buds and dietary requirements.

In this cookbook, we hope to walk you through each stage of your Ninja Creami adventure. We've got you covered, from setting up your machine and learning about its capabilities to mastering the fundamentals of frozen dessert manufacturing. We believe that the best way to learn is to do, which is why we've included a selection of recipes that will teach you the fundamentals of creating ice cream, sorbet, gelato, and more, while also pushing you to explore and create your own unique flavors.

Before you go into the delectable world of homemade frozen desserts, be sure you're familiar with your Ninja Creami. We'll go over everything from unboxing and setup to understanding the various functions and settings that make the Ninja Creami such a useful tool in the kitchen. Safety rules and maintenance tips help guarantee that your machine runs smoothly and efficiently every time you use it. Making the perfect frozen treat requires both art and science. We'll look at the science behind what makes ice cream creamy, sorbets refreshing, and gelato rich in taste. Understanding the role of each ingredient and how they interact during the freezing process will allow you to customize recipes and even build your own from start.

There is more to the Ninja Creami than simply following recipes. We'll provide vital tips and tactics to help you get the ideal texture and flavor in every batch. From selecting the best base and mix-ins to troubleshooting frequent problems, you'll learn how to get the most out of your Ninja Creami.

Remember that cooking frozen desserts should be both enjoyable and fulfilling. Don't be afraid to try, fail, and learn as you go. The Ninja Creami Cookbook for Beginners is more than simply a recipe book; it's a resource to help you unleash your creativity and enthusiasm for homemade frozen desserts.

So, let's turn the page and embark on this delightful adventure together. Your Ninja Creami is ready to transform your frozen dreams into creamy realities!

Chapter 1
Understanding Your Ninja Creami: Features and Functions

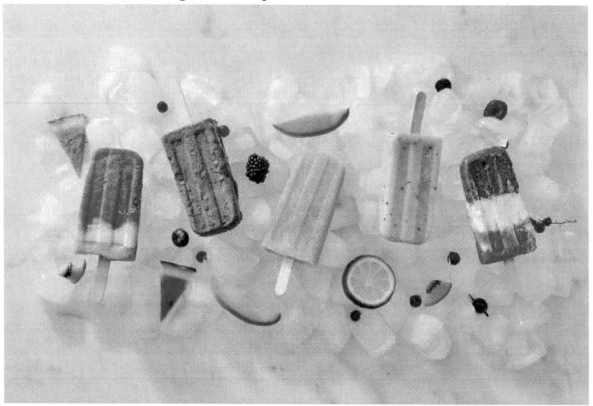

The Ninja Creami transforms the ice cream-making experience at home, providing unrivaled control and variety in creating the ideal frozen desserts. To effectively utilize its powers, familiarize yourself with its features and operations. This chapter will walk you through the different parts of the Ninja Creami, explaining how each function works and how to utilize them to make delicious, creamy delights.

The Essentials of Your Ninja Creami

Your Ninja Creami includes a number of critical components, each of which is meant to simplify the process of preparing frozen desserts. The Ninja Creami is made up of three parts: a base with the engine and controls, a removable pint container for freezing desserts, and the Creamerizer™ paddle, which converts frozen blocks into creamy pleasures.

Key Features:

• Multiple pre-set programs: The Ninja Creami comes with many pre-set programs for various sorts of frozen desserts, such as ice cream, gelato, sorbet, smoothie bowls, and even dairy-free alternatives. Each program is intended to produce the best texture for the specific dessert type.

• Re-spin Function: Occasionally, the original spin may not achieve the desired uniformity. The re-spin option allows you to process your mixture again, resulting in a smoother, more uniform texture.

• Manual Mode: Customize the texture to your preferences by controlling the processing time.

Understanding the Control Panel

The control panel is your interface for maximizing the performance of your Ninja Creami. It has buttons for each pre-set program, the manual mode, and the start/stop function. Some models may also have a digital display that shows the selected program and provides reminders and timers throughout the process.

Pre-Set Programs Explained

Each pre-set program is designed to handle the mixture in a way that maximizes the texture and consistency for the particular type of dessert. Here's a quick overview:

• Ice Cream: Produces creamy, scoopable ice cream.

• Gelato is a rich, delicious treat made with less air than regular ice cream.

• Sorbet: A fruit-based frozen delicacy that is both refreshing and light.

• Smoothie Bowl: Ideal for thicker, spoonable smoothies with optional toppings.

• Dairy-Free: Specifically designed for non-dairy bases, resulting in a creamy texture without using milk or cream.

Optimizing Your Ninja Creami's Potential

To make the most of your Ninja Creami, consider the following suggestions:

• Experiment with ingredients. The Ninja Creami's adaptability allows you to experiment with a wide variety of ingredients, including standard cream bases, unusual fruits, and even vegan alternatives.

• Use Re-Spin Wisely: If your dessert doesn't reach the appropriate consistency after the initial spin, use the re-spin feature. Sometimes a second spin can make all the difference.

• Use Manual Mode for Custom Creations: Fine-tune your dessert texture. This is especially useful for producing distinctive textures or inserting delicate mix-ins that may be harmed by normal programs.

• Keep your pint container frozen. For optimal results, make sure your pint container is completely frozen before use. A well frozen container is necessary for achieving the desired texture.

Understanding the capabilities and functionalities of the Ninja Creami allows you to create a variety of frozen desserts. With this information, you're ready to try the dishes in this cookbook and even create your own bespoke creations. Whether you want a classic vanilla ice cream, a refreshing sorbet, or a rich and creamy gelato, your Ninja Creami is ready to fulfill your frozen dessert wishes.

Getting started: Setup and Safety Guidelines

Setting up your Ninja Creami and following safety rules are critical steps toward a smooth and joyful ice cream-making experience. Here's how to get started while keeping safety in mind.

Initial Setup

1. Unboxing the Ninja Creami: Carefully remove the Ninja Creami and all of its components from their packing. Check the user handbook to confirm that all components are present.

2. Before use, wash the removable parts (pint container, lid, and Creamerizer™ paddle) with warm soapy water. These parts are also dishwasher-safe for your convenience. Wipe down the base with a moist towel, but do not submerge it in water.

3. Assembly: Insert the clean and dry pint container into the Ninja Creami base. Attach the Creamerizer™ paddle to the lid and securely close the pint container.

Safety Guidelines

1. Read the manual. Before using your Ninja Creami, make sure you understand the manufacturer's instructions and safety information.

2. Place the Ninja Creami on a firm, flat surface away from water and heat.

3. To ensure electrical safety, plug the gadget directly into a wall socket. To avoid

electrical risks, don't use extension cords.

4. Always supervise when using the Ninja Creami. Keep the appliance out of children's reach.

5. Handle the Blade: The Creamerizer™ paddle is sharp. Handle it with caution, particularly when cleaning.

6. Don't overfill the pint container. Allow enough space for the mixture to expand while freezing.

7. Cool hot ingredients to room temperature before freezing in pint containers.

Tips for Making Perfect Ice Cream Every Time

Creating the ideal ice cream with your Ninja Creami is an art that requires practice. Here are some tips and tactics that will help you obtain the greatest outcomes.

1. To achieve a smoother texture, chill your ice cream base in the fridge for at least 4 hours or overnight before freezing in a pint container. This helps to reduce ice crystal formation.

2. Use high-quality, fresh ingredients for optimal flavor. The taste of your ice cream will be directly proportional to the quality of the ingredients utilized.

3. Follow balanced recipes, especially when beginning out. The mix of sugar, fat, and liquid is critical to texture and flavor.

4. To make creamy ice cream, put your Ninja Creami to the proper mode that incorporates air into the mixture while freezing and spinning.

5. Add Mix-Ins Later: To uniformly distribute mix-ins like chocolate chips or nuts, add them in the last few minutes of spinning to avoid breaking them down.

6. Store ice cream in an airtight container to avoid freezer burn. Before sealing the container, press a piece of parchment paper directly onto the ice cream's surface.

5. The Science of Frozen Desserts: How Ninja Creami Changed the Game

The Ninja Creami's revolutionary approach to texture and consistency transforms the process of preparing frozen dessert. Understanding the science behind it can help you improve your ice cream-making skills.

Freezing and Churning

Traditional ice cream makers freeze and churn the mixture simultaneously, resulting in varying textures. The Ninja Creami, on the other hand, begins with a frozen solid block that is then shaved and churned to provide a consistent, creamy texture every time.

Control Over Crystal Size

Ice cream's texture is heavily influenced by the size of the ice crystals created during the freezing process. Smaller crystals result in a smoother texture. The Ninja Creami's innovative method produces evenly little ice crystals, yielding incredibly smooth ice cream.

Air is a key role in the texture of frozen desserts. The Ninja Creami effectively mixes air into the mixture during the spinning phase, resulting in a light and creamy texture reminiscent of the best commercial ice creams.

Versatile and creative

The ability to begin with a frozen block allows for limitless inventiveness. You can freeze a wide range of bases, including dairy and fruit purees, and then turn them into ice cream, sorbets, or gelatos. This method also makes it easier to experiment with sugar substitutions and non-dairy options while maintaining texture.

Understanding and using your Ninja Creami's features and functionalities, as well as following these setup, safety, and usage instructions, will get you on your way to generating a diverse selection of frozen delicacies to suit all tastes and dietary needs. Enjoy the process of trying and honing your abilities as you discover the delectable possibilities that your Ninja Creami provides.

Vanilla Bean Lite Ice Cream

Prep Time: 10 minutes
Cook Time: N/A
Serving Size: 2 servings
Ingredients:

- 2 cups skim milk
- 1/2 cup granulated sugar substitute
- 1 tsp vanilla bean paste
- Pinch of salt

Instructions:

1. Mix all ingredients in a bowl until the sugar substitute is fully dissolved.
2. Pour the mixture into the Ninja Creami pint container and freeze for 24 hours.
3. Follow the Ninja Creami instructions for Ice Cream setting.
4. Enjoy immediately for a soft-serve texture or freeze for 2 hours for a firmer consistency.

Nutritional Information (per serving):
Calories: 120 | Fat: 0g | Carbohydrates: 18g | Protein: 8g

Chocolate Lite Ice Cream

Prep Time: 10 minutes
Cook Time: N/A
Serving Size: 2 servings
Ingredients:

- 2 cups almond milk, unsweetened
- 1/2 cup cocoa powder
- 1/2 cup granulated sugar substitute
- 1 tsp vanilla extract

Instructions:

1. Whisk together all ingredients until smooth and the sugar substitute is dissolved.

2. Transfer to the Ninja Creami pint container and freeze solid, about 24 hours.

3. Process using the Ice Cream function.

4. Serve immediately or freeze for a firmer texture.

Nutritional Information (per serving):
Calories: 100 | Fat: 3g | Carbohydrates: 15g | Protein: 5g

Strawberry Lite Ice Cream

Prep Time: 15 minutes
Cook Time: N/A
Serving Size: 2 servings
Ingredients:

*   2 cups frozen strawberries

*   1 cup Greek yogurt, non-fat

*   1/2 cup granulated sugar substitute

*   1 tsp lemon juice

Instructions:

1. Blend strawberries, Greek yogurt, sugar substitute, and lemon juice until smooth.

2. Pour into the Ninja Creami pint container and freeze for 24 hours.

3. Use the Ice Cream setting to process.

4. Serve immediately for a soft texture or freeze for a firmer consistency.

Nutritional Information (per serving):
Calories: 130 | Fat: 0g | Carbohydrates: 17g | Protein: 12g

Mint Chip Lite Ice Cream

Prep Time: 10 minutes
Cook Time: N/A
Serving Size: 2 servings
Ingredients:

- 2 cups skim milk

- 1/2 cup granulated sugar substitute

- 1 tsp mint extract

- 1/4 cup dark chocolate chips, sugar-free

Instructions:

1. Combine skim milk, sugar substitute, and mint extract; stir until dissolved.

2. Freeze in the Ninja Creami pint container for 24 hours.

3. Process using the Ice Cream setting, then add chocolate chips and use the Mix-In feature.

4. Enjoy immediately or freeze for additional firmness.

Nutritional Information (per serving):
Calories: 150 | Fat: 5g | Carbohydrates: 18g | Protein: 8g

Peach Lite Ice Cream

Prep Time: 15 minutes
Cook Time: N/A
Serving Size: 2 servings
Ingredients:

- 2 cups frozen peaches

- 1 cup Greek yogurt, non-fat

- 1/2 cup granulated sugar substitute

- 1 tsp vanilla extract

Instructions:

1. Blend all ingredients until smooth.

2. Freeze in the Ninja Creami pint container for 24 hours.

3. Process using the Ice Cream setting.

4. Serve soft or freeze for a firmer texture.

Nutritional Information (per serving):
Calories: 130 | Fat: 0g | Carbohydrates: 19g | Protein: 12g

Coffee Lite Ice Cream

Prep Time: 10 minutes
Cook Time: N/A
Serving Size: 2 servings
Ingredients:

- 2 cups almond milk, unsweetened

- 1/2 cup strong brewed coffee, cooled

- 1/2 cup granulated sugar substitute

- 1 tsp vanilla extract

Instructions:

1. Mix all ingredients until the sugar substitute dissolves.

2. Pour into the Ninja Creami pint container and freeze for 24 hours.

3. Use the Ice Cream function to process.

4. Serve immediately for a soft texture or freeze for a firmer consistency.

Nutritional Information (per serving):
Calories: 60 | Fat: 2g | Carbohydrates: 8g | Protein: 1g

Lemon Curd Lite Ice Cream

Prep Time: 15 minutes
Cook Time: N/A
Serving Size: 2 servings
Ingredients:

- 2 cups Greek yogurt, non-fat

- 1/2 cup lemon curd, sugar-free

- 1 tsp lemon zest

Instructions:

1. Mix Greek yogurt with lemon curd and zest until well combined.

2. Freeze in the Ninja Creami pint container for 24 hours.

3. Process using the Ice Cream setting.

4. Serve immediately for a soft consistency or freeze for a firmer ice cream.

Nutritional Information (per serving):
Calories: 140 | Fat: 0g | Carbohydrates: 20g | Protein: 13g

Raspberry Ripple Lite Ice Cream

Prep Time: 20 minutes
Cook Time: N/A
Serving Size: 2 servings
Ingredients:

- 2 cups Greek yogurt, non-fat

- 1/2 cup granulated sugar substitute

- 1 cup raspberries, mashed

- 1 tsp vanilla extract

Instructions:

1. Mix Greek yogurt, sugar substitute, and vanilla extract.

2. Layer the yogurt mixture and mashed raspberries in the Ninja Creami pint container, then swirl lightly with a knife.

3. Freeze for 24 hours.

4. Process using the Ice Cream setting.

5. Serve immediately or freeze for a firmer texture.

Nutritional Information (per serving):
Calories: 130 | Fat: 0g | Carbohydrates: 18g | Protein: 13g

Coconut Lime Lite Ice Cream

Prep Time: 10 minutes
Cook Time: N/A
Serving Size: 2 servings
Ingredients:

- 2 cups coconut milk, light

- 1/2 cup granulated sugar substitute

- 1 tbsp lime juice

- 1 tsp lime zest

Instructions:

1. Whisk together coconut milk, sugar substitute, lime juice, and zest until well combined.

2. Freeze in the Ninja Creami pint container for 24 hours.

3. Use the Ice Cream setting to process.

4. Enjoy immediately or freeze for a firmer consistency.

Nutritional Information (per serving):
Calories: 100 | Fat: 5g | Carbohydrates: 13g | Protein: 1g

Banana Nut Lite Ice Cream

Prep Time: 15 minutes
Cook Time: N/A
Serving Size: 2 servings
Ingredients:

- 2 ripe bananas, frozen
- 1 cup almond milk, unsweetened
- 1/2 cup granulated sugar substitute
- 1/4 cup walnuts, chopped
- 1 tsp vanilla extract

Instructions:

1. Blend bananas, almond milk, sugar substitute, and vanilla extract until smooth.
2. Stir in walnuts.
3. Freeze in the Ninja Creami pint container for 24 hours.
4. Process using the Ice Cream setting, adding walnuts through the Mix-In feature if desired.
5. Serve immediately or freeze for a firmer texture.

Nutritional Information (per serving):
Calories: 180 | Fat: 8g | Carbohydrates: 24g | Protein: 4g

Classic Cookies and Cream Ice Cream

Prep Time: 15 minutes
Cook Time: N/A
Serving Size: 2 servings
Ingredients:

- 2 cups heavy cream

- 1 cup whole milk

- 3/4 cup granulated sugar

- 1 tbsp vanilla extract

- 1 cup crushed chocolate sandwich cookies

Instructions:

1. Combine heavy cream, milk, sugar, and vanilla in a bowl and stir until sugar dissolves.

2. Pour into the Ninja Creami pint container and freeze for 24 hours.

3. Use the Ice Cream setting to process.

4. Add crushed cookies using the Mix-In function.

5. Serve immediately or freeze for a firmer texture.

Nutritional Information (per serving):
Calories: 500 | Fat: 30g | Carbohydrates: 50g | Protein: 5g

Mint Chocolate Chip Ice Cream

Prep Time: 15 minutes
Cook Time: N/A
Serving Size: 2 servings
Ingredients:

- 2 cups heavy cream

- 1 cup whole milk

- 3/4 cup granulated sugar

- 1 tsp mint extract

- 1/2 cup mini chocolate chips

Instructions:

1. Mix cream, milk, sugar, and mint extract until sugar is dissolved.

2. Freeze in the Ninja Creami pint container for 24 hours.

3. Process using the Ice Cream setting.

4. Mix in chocolate chips using the Mix-In function.

5. Serve immediately for soft-serve or freeze for a firmer consistency.

Nutritional Information (per serving):
Calories: 530 | Fat: 35g | Carbohydrates: 52g | Protein: 5g

Salted Caramel Pretzel Ice Cream
Prep Time: 15 minutes
Cook Time: N/A
Serving Size: 2 servings
Ingredients:

- 2 cups heavy cream

- 1 cup whole milk

- 3/4 cup granulated sugar

- 1/2 cup salted caramel sauce

- 1 cup crushed pretzels

Instructions:

1. Combine cream, milk, and sugar, stirring until the sugar dissolves.

2. Stir in the caramel sauce.

3. Freeze in the Ninja Creami pint container for 24 hours.

4. Process using the Ice Cream setting.

5. Add crushed pretzels using the Mix-In function.

6. Enjoy immediately or freeze for a firmer texture.

Nutritional Information (per serving):
Calories: 600 | Fat: 40g | Carbohydrates: 58g | Protein: 8g

Rocky Road Ice Cream

Prep Time: 15 minutes
Cook Time: N/A
Serving Size: 2 servings
Ingredients:

- 2 cups heavy cream
- 1 cup whole milk
- 3/4 cup granulated sugar
- 1/2 cup cocoa powder
- 1/2 cup mini marshmallows
- 1/2 cup chopped almonds

Instructions:

1. Whisk together cream, milk, sugar, and cocoa until smooth.

2. Freeze in the Ninja Creami pint container for 24 hours.

3. Process using the Ice Cream setting.

4. Add marshmallows and almonds using the Mix-In function.

5. Serve immediately or freeze for a firmer consistency.

Nutritional Information (per serving):
Calories: 560 | Fat: 40g | Carbohydrates: 48g | Protein: 10g

Birthday Cake Ice Cream

Prep Time: 20 minutes
Cook Time: N/A
Serving Size: 2 servings
Ingredients:

- 2 cups heavy cream

- 1 cup whole milk

- 3/4 cup granulated sugar

- 1 tbsp vanilla extract

- 1/2 cup rainbow sprinkles

- 1/2 cup cake mix

Instructions:

1. Mix cream, milk, sugar, and vanilla until sugar dissolves.

2. Stir in cake mix until well combined.

3. Freeze in the Ninja Creami pint container for 24 hours.

4. Process using the Ice Cream setting.

5. Mix in rainbow sprinkles using the Mix-In function.

6. Enjoy immediately or freeze for a firmer consistency.

Nutritional Information (per serving):
Calories: 580 | Fat: 35g | Carbohydrates: 62g | Protein: 5g

Peanut Butter Cup Ice Cream

Prep Time: 15 minutes
Cook Time: N/A
Serving Size: 2 servings
Ingredients:

- 2 cups heavy cream

- 1 cup whole milk

- 3/4 cup granulated sugar

- 1/2 cup peanut butter, smooth

- 1 cup chopped peanut butter cups

Instructions:

1. Combine cream, milk, and sugar, stirring until sugar dissolves.

2. Mix in peanut butter until smooth.

3. Freeze in the Ninja Creami pint container for 24 hours.

4. Process using the Ice Cream setting.

5. Add chopped peanut butter cups using the Mix-In function.

6. Serve immediately or freeze for additional firmness.

Nutritional Information (per serving):

Calories: 650 | Fat: 45g | Carbohydrates: 55g | Protein: 15g

S'mores Ice Cream

Prep Time: 20 minutes
Cook Time: N/A
Serving Size: 2 servings
Ingredients:

- 2 cups heavy cream

- 1 cup whole milk

- 3/4 cup granulated sugar

- 1/2 cup chocolate chips

- 1/2 cup crushed graham crackers

- 1/2 cup mini marshmallows

Instructions:

1. Mix heavy cream, milk, and sugar until the sugar is fully dissolved.

2. Freeze in the Ninja Creami pint container for 24 hours.

3. Use the Ice Cream setting to process the frozen base.

4. Add chocolate chips, crushed graham crackers, and mini marshmallows using the Mix-In function.

5. Serve immediately for a soft texture or freeze for a more traditional ice cream consistency.

Nutritional Information (per serving):
Calories: 570 | Fat: 35g | Carbohydrates: 60g | Protein: 7g

Coffee Toffee Ice Cream

Prep Time: 15 minutes
Cook Time: N/A
Serving Size: 2 servings
Ingredients:

- 2 cups heavy cream

- 1 cup whole milk

- 3/4 cup granulated sugar

- 2 tbsp instant coffee granules

- 1/2 cup toffee bits

Instructions:

1. Dissolve the instant coffee in a small amount of hot water and let cool.

2. Combine the coffee mixture with cream, milk, and sugar, stirring until the sugar is dissolved.

3. Freeze in the Ninja Creami pint container for 24 hours.

4. Process using the Ice Cream setting.

5. Add toffee bits using the Mix-In function.

6. Enjoy immediately or freeze for a firmer texture.

Nutritional Information (per serving):
Calories: 560 | Fat: 38g | Carbohydrates: 52g | Protein: 5g

Strawberry Cheesecake Ice Cream

Prep Time: 20 minutes
Cook Time: N/A
Serving Size: 2 servings
Ingredients:

- 2 cups heavy cream

- 1 cup whole milk

- 3/4 cup granulated sugar

- 1/2 cup cream cheese, softened

- 1 tsp vanilla extract

- 1 cup fresh strawberries, chopped

- 1/2 cup graham cracker crumbs

Instructions:

1. Blend cream cheese, cream, milk, sugar, and vanilla until smooth.

2. Stir in chopped strawberries.

3. Freeze in the Ninja Creami pint container for 24 hours.

4. Process using the Ice Cream setting.

5. Add graham cracker crumbs using the Mix-In function.

6. Serve immediately or freeze for a firmer consistency.

Nutritional Information (per serving):
Calories: 580 | Fat: 40g | Carbohydrates: 52g | Protein: 7g

Chocolate Fudge Brownie Ice Cream

Prep Time: 15 minutes
Cook Time: N/A
Serving Size: 2 servings
Ingredients:

- 2 cups heavy cream

- 1 cup whole milk

- 3/4 cup granulated sugar

- 1/2 cup cocoa powder

- 1 cup brownie chunks

Instructions:

1. Whisk together cream, milk, sugar, and cocoa powder until the sugar and cocoa are dissolved.

2. Freeze in the Ninja Creami pint container for 24 hours.

3. Process using the Ice Cream setting.

4. Add brownie chunks using the Mix-In function.

5. Serve immediately for a soft-serve texture or freeze for a firmer consistency.

Nutritional Information (per serving):
Calories: 600 | Fat: 38g | Carbohydrates: 58g | Protein: 8g

Vanilla Bean Ice Cream

Prep Time: 10 minutes
Cook Time: N/A
Serving Size: 4 servings
Ingredients:

- 2 cups heavy cream

- 1 cup whole milk

- 3/4 cup granulated sugar

- 1 vanilla bean, split and scraped

Instructions:

1. Combine cream, milk, sugar, and the seeds from the vanilla bean in a bowl. Stir until the sugar dissolves completely.

2. Pour the mixture into the Ninja Creami pint container and freeze for 24 hours.

3. Process using the Ice Cream setting.

4. Serve immediately or freeze for a firmer consistency.

Nutritional Information (per serving):
Calories: 450 | Fat: 30g | Carbohydrates: 40g | Protein: 3g

Chocolate Ice Cream

Prep Time: 10 minutes
Cook Time: N/A
Serving Size: 4 servings
Ingredients:

- 2 cups heavy cream

- 1 cup whole milk

- 3/4 cup granulated sugar

- 1/2 cup unsweetened cocoa powder

Instructions:

1. Whisk together cream, milk, sugar, and cocoa powder until well blended and sugar is dissolved.

2. Freeze in the Ninja Creami pint container for 24 hours.

3. Use the Ice Cream setting to process.

4. Enjoy immediately for a soft serve texture or freeze for a firmer ice cream.

Nutritional Information (per serving):
Calories: 460 | Fat: 32g | Carbohydrates: 42g | Protein: 5g

Strawberry Ice Cream

Prep Time: 15 minutes
Cook Time: N/A
Serving Size: 4 servings
Ingredients:

- 2 cups heavy cream

- 1 cup whole milk

- 3/4 cup granulated sugar

- 1 cup strawberries, pureed

Instructions:

1. Blend cream, milk, sugar, and strawberry puree until smooth.

2. Freeze in the Ninja Creami pint container for 24 hours.

3. Process using the Ice Cream setting.

4. Serve immediately or freeze for a firmer texture.

Nutritional Information (per serving):
Calories: 440 | Fat: 30g | Carbohydrates: 40g | Protein: 3g

Mint Chocolate Chip Ice Cream

Prep Time: 10 minutes
Cook Time: N/A
Serving Size: 4 servings
Ingredients:

- 2 cups heavy cream

- 1 cup whole milk

- 3/4 cup granulated sugar

- 1 tsp mint extract

- 1/2 cup mini chocolate chips

Instructions:

1. Mix cream, milk, sugar, and mint extract until the sugar is dissolved.

2. Stir in chocolate chips.

3. Freeze in the Ninja Creami pint container for 24 hours.

4. Process using the Ice Cream setting.

5. Serve immediately for a soft texture or freeze for a traditional ice cream consistency.

Nutritional Information (per serving):
Calories: 530 | Fat: 35g | Carbohydrates: 52g | Protein: 5g

Coffee Ice Cream

Prep Time: 10 minutes
Cook Time: N/A
Serving Size: 4 servings
Ingredients:

- 2 cups heavy cream

- 1 cup whole milk

- 3/4 cup granulated sugar

- 2 tbsp instant coffee granules, dissolved in 1 tbsp hot water

Instructions:

1. Combine cream, milk, sugar, and dissolved coffee in a bowl. Stir until sugar is fully dissolved.

2. Transfer to the Ninja Creami pint container and freeze for 24 hours.

3. Process using the Ice Cream setting.

4. Serve immediately for a creamy texture or freeze for a firmer consistency.

Nutritional Information (per serving):
Calories: 450 | Fat: 32g | Carbohydrates: 40g | Protein: 3g

Pistachio Ice Cream

Prep Time: 15 minutes
Cook Time: N/A
Serving Size: 4 servings
Ingredients:

- 2 cups heavy cream

- 1 cup whole milk

- 3/4 cup granulated sugar

- 1/2 cup pistachio paste

Instructions:

1. Whisk together cream, milk, sugar, and pistachio paste until well combined.

2. Freeze in the Ninja Creami pint container for 24 hours.

3. Process using the Ice Cream setting.

4. Serve immediately or freeze for a firmer texture.

Nutritional Information (per serving):
Calories: 480 | Fat: 34g | Carbohydrates: 40g | Protein: 6g

Caramel Swirl Ice Cream

Prep Time: 10 minutes
Cook Time: N/A
Serving Size: 4 servings
Ingredients:

- 2 cups heavy cream

- 1 cup whole milk

- 3/4 cup granulated sugar

- 1/2 cup caramel sauce

Instructions:

1. Mix cream, milk, and sugar until sugar dissolves.

2. Pour mixture into the Ninja Creami pint container, leaving a little space for the caramel.

3. Drizzle caramel sauce over the top and use a knife to gently swirl it into the mixture.

4. Freeze for 24 hours.

5. Process using the Ice Cream setting.

6. Serve immediately for a soft serve texture or freeze for a more traditional ice cream texture.

Nutritional Information (per serving):
Calories: 520 | Fat: 35g | Carbohydrates: 52g | Protein: 3g

Peach Ice Cream

Prep Time: 15 minutes
Cook Time: N/A
Serving Size: 4 servings
Ingredients:

- 2 cups heavy cream

- 1 cup whole milk

- 3/4 cup granulated sugar

- 1 cup peaches, pureed

Instructions:

1. Blend cream, milk, sugar, and peach puree until smooth.

2. Freeze in the Ninja Creami pint container for 24 hours.

3. Process using the Ice Cream setting.

4. Serve immediately or freeze for a firmer consistency.

Nutritional Information (per serving):
Calories: 440 | Fat: 30g | Carbohydrates: 40g | Protein: 3g

Lemon Curd Ice Cream

Prep Time: 10 minutes
Cook Time: N/A
Serving Size: 4 servings
Ingredients:

- 2 cups heavy cream

- 1 cup whole milk

- 3/4 cup granulated sugar

- 1/2 cup lemon curd

Instructions:

1. Mix cream, milk, sugar, and lemon curd until well combined.

2. Freeze in the Ninja Creami pint container for 24 hours.

3. Process using the Ice Cream setting.

4. Serve immediately for a soft texture or freeze for a firmer consistency.

Nutritional Information (per serving):
Calories: 470 | Fat: 32g | Carbohydrates: 42g | Protein: 3g

Raspberry Ripple Ice Cream

Prep Time: 15 minutes
Cook Time: N/A
Serving Size: 4 servings
Ingredients:

- 2 cups heavy cream

- 1 cup whole milk

- 3/4 cup granulated sugar

- 1/2 cup raspberry puree

- 1/4 cup raspberry jam

Instructions:

1. Combine cream, milk, and sugar in a bowl. Stir until sugar dissolves.

2. Mix in the raspberry puree.

3. Pour the mixture into the Ninja Creami pint container and freeze for 24 hours.

4. After processing with the Ice Cream setting, layer the ice cream with dollops of raspberry jam, gently swirling with a knife.

5. Serve immediately for a soft texture or freeze for a traditional ice cream consistency.

Nutritional Information (per serving):
Calories: 460 | Fat: 32g | Carbohydrates: 44g | Protein: 3g

Classic Vanilla Gelato

Prep Time: 10 minutes
Cook Time: N/A
Serving Size: 4 servings
Ingredients:

- 2 cups whole milk

- 1 cup heavy cream

- 3/4 cup granulated sugar

- 1 vanilla bean, split and scraped, or 2 tsp vanilla extract

Instructions:

1. Combine milk, cream, sugar, and vanilla in a bowl, stirring until the sugar is fully dissolved.

2. Pour the mixture into the Ninja Creami pint container and freeze for 24 hours.

3. Process using the Gelato setting.

4. Serve immediately for a creamy texture or freeze for a firmer consistency.

Nutritional Information (per serving):
Calories: 350 | Fat: 22g | Carbohydrates: 34g | Protein: 4g

Rich Chocolate Gelato

Prep Time: 10 minutes
Cook Time: N/A
Serving Size: 4 servings
Ingredients:

- 2 cups whole milk

- 1 cup heavy cream

- 3/4 cup granulated sugar

- 1/2 cup unsweetened cocoa powder

Instructions:

1. Whisk together milk, cream, sugar, and cocoa powder until the sugar and cocoa are fully dissolved.

2. Freeze in the Ninja Creami pint container for 24 hours.

3. Use the Gelato setting to process.

4. Enjoy immediately for a soft texture or freeze for a firmer gelato.

Nutritional Information (per serving):
Calories: 360 | Fat: 22g | Carbohydrates: 36g | Protein: 5g

Pistachio Gelato

Prep Time: 15 minutes
Cook Time: N/A
Serving Size: 4 servings
Ingredients:

- 2 cups whole milk

- 1 cup heavy cream

- 3/4 cup granulated sugar

- 1/2 cup pistachio paste

Instructions:

1. Blend milk, cream, sugar, and pistachio paste until smooth.

2. Freeze in the Ninja Creami pint container for 24 hours.

3. Process using the Gelato setting.

4. Serve immediately or freeze for a firmer texture.

Nutritional Information (per serving):
Calories: 380 | Fat: 24g | Carbohydrates: 36g | Protein: 6g

Strawberry Gelato

Prep Time: 15 minutes
Cook Time: N/A
Serving Size: 4 servings
Ingredients:

- 2 cups whole milk

- 1 cup heavy cream

- 3/4 cup granulated sugar

- 1 cup strawberries, pureed

Instructions:

1. Mix milk, cream, sugar, and strawberry puree until the sugar dissolves.

2. Pour into the Ninja Creami pint container and freeze for 24 hours.

3. Process using the Gelato setting.

4. Serve immediately or freeze for a firmer consistency.

Nutritional Information (per serving):
Calories: 350 | Fat: 22g | Carbohydrates: 36g | Protein: 4g

Hazelnut Gelato

Prep Time: 15 minutes
Cook Time: N/A
Serving Size: 4 servings
Ingredients:

- 2 cups whole milk

- 1 cup heavy cream

- 3/4 cup granulated sugar

- 1/2 cup hazelnut paste

Instructions:

1. Whisk together milk, cream, sugar, and hazelnut paste until well combined.

2. Freeze in the Ninja Creami pint container for 24 hours.

3. Process using the Gelato setting.

4. Serve immediately for a soft, creamy texture or freeze for a firmer consistency.

Nutritional Information (per serving):
Calories: 380 | Fat: 24g | Carbohydrates: 36g | Protein: 5g

Coffee Gelato

Prep Time: 10 minutes
Cook Time: N/A
Serving Size: 4 servings
Ingredients:

- 2 cups whole milk

- 1 cup heavy cream

- 3/4 cup granulated sugar

- 2 tbsp instant coffee granules, dissolved in 1 tbsp hot water

Instructions:

1. Combine milk, cream, sugar, and dissolved coffee in a bowl, stirring until the sugar is fully dissolved.

2. Transfer to the Ninja Creami pint container and freeze for 24 hours.

3. Process using the Gelato setting.

4. Serve immediately or freeze for a firmer texture.

Nutritional Information (per serving):
Calories: 350 | Fat: 22g | Carbohydrates: 34g | Protein: 4g

7. Lemon Gelato

Prep Time: 10 minutes
Cook Time: N/A
Serving Size: 4 servings
Ingredients:

- 2 cups whole milk

- 1 cup heavy cream

- 3/4 cup granulated sugar

- 1/2 cup fresh lemon juice

- Zest of 2 lemons

Instructions:

1. Mix milk, cream, sugar, lemon juice, and zest until the sugar is dissolved.

2. Pour into the Ninja Creami pint container and freeze for 24 hours.

3. Use the Gelato setting to process.

4. Enjoy immediately for a refreshing, creamy texture or freeze for later.

Nutritional Information (per serving):
Calories: 350 | Fat: 22g | Carbohydrates: 35g | Protein: 4g

Mango Gelato
Prep Time: 15 minutes
Cook Time: N/A
Serving Size: 4 servings
Ingredients:

- 2 cups whole milk

- 1 cup heavy cream

- 3/4 cup granulated sugar

- 1 cup mango puree

Instructions:

1. Blend milk, cream, sugar, and mango puree until smooth.

2. Freeze in the Ninja Creami pint container for 24 hours.

3. Process using the Gelato setting.

4. Serve immediately for a tropical treat or freeze for later enjoyment.

Nutritional Information (per serving):
Calories: 350 | Fat: 22g | Carbohydrates: 36g | Protein: 4g

Tiramisu Gelato

Prep Time: 20 minutes
Cook Time: N/A
Serving Size: 4 servings
Ingredients:

- 2 cups whole milk

- 1 cup heavy cream

- 3/4 cup granulated sugar

- 1/2 cup mascarpone cheese

- 2 tbsp espresso or strong coffee

- 1/4 cup cocoa powder for dusting

Instructions:

1. Whisk together milk, cream, sugar, mascarpone, and espresso until smooth.

2. Freeze in the Ninja Creami pint container for 24 hours.

3. Process using the Gelato setting.

4. Dust with cocoa powder before serving for an authentic tiramisu flavor.

Nutritional Information (per serving):
Calories: 420 | Fat: 28g | Carbohydrates: 38g | Protein: 6g

10. Cinnamon Gelato

Prep Time: 10 minutes
Cook Time: N/A
Serving Size: 4 servings
Ingredients:

- 2 cups whole milk

- 1 cup heavy cream

- 3/4 cup granulated sugar

- 1 tbsp ground cinnamon

Instructions:

1. Combine all ingredients in a bowl and mix until the sugar has dissolved.

2. Transfer to the Ninja Creami pint container and freeze for 24 hours.

3. Use the Gelato setting to process.

4. Serve immediately for a spiced, creamy delight or freeze for later.

Nutritional Information (per serving):

Calories: 350 | Fat: 22g | Carbohydrates: 35g | Protein: 4g

Classic Lemon Sorbet

Prep Time: 10 minutes
Cook Time: N/A
Serving Size: 4 servings
Ingredients:

- 1 cup water

- 3/4 cup granulated sugar

- 1 cup fresh lemon juice

- Zest of 1 lemon

Instructions:

1. In a saucepan over medium heat, dissolve sugar in water to create a simple syrup. Let cool.

2. Stir in lemon juice and zest to the cooled syrup.

3. Pour the mixture into the Ninja Creami pint container and freeze for 24 hours.

4. Process using the Sorbet setting.

5. Serve immediately for a refreshing treat or store in the freezer.

Nutritional Information (per serving):
Calories: 180 | Fat: 0g | Carbohydrates: 46g | Protein: 0g

Mango Lime Sorbet

Prep Time: 15 minutes
Cook Time: N/A
Serving Size: 4 servings
Ingredients:

- 1 cup water

- 3/4 cup granulated sugar

- 2 cups mango puree

- Juice of 1 lime

Instructions:

1. Make a simple syrup by dissolving sugar in water over medium heat. Allow to cool.

2. Mix the mango puree and lime juice into the cooled syrup.

3. Freeze in the Ninja Creami pint container for 24 hours.

4. Use the Sorbet setting to process.

5. Enjoy immediately or freeze for later use.

Nutritional Information (per serving):
Calories: 200 | Fat: 0g | Carbohydrates: 51g | Protein: 1g

Raspberry Sorbet
Prep Time: 10 minutes
Cook Time: N/A
Serving Size: 4 servings
Ingredients:

- 1 cup water

- 3/4 cup granulated sugar

- 3 cups fresh raspberries

Instructions:

1. Create a simple syrup by heating sugar and water until sugar is dissolved. Cool to room temperature.

2. Puree raspberries and strain to remove seeds.

3. Mix raspberry puree with the simple syrup.

4. Freeze in the Ninja Creami pint container for 24 hours.

5. Process using the Sorbet setting.

6. Serve immediately for a burst of berry flavor or store in the freezer.

Nutritional Information (per serving):
Calories: 190 | Fat: 0g | Carbohydrates: 48g | Protein: 1g

Peach Basil Sorbet

Prep Time: 15 minutes
Cook Time: N/A
Serving Size: 4 servings
Ingredients:

- 1 cup water

- 3/4 cup granulated sugar

- 2 cups peach puree

- 1/4 cup fresh basil leaves, finely chopped

Instructions:

1. Dissolve sugar in water over medium heat to make a simple syrup. Let it cool.

2. Combine peach puree and chopped basil with the cooled syrup.

3. Pour into the Ninja Creami pint container and freeze for 24 hours.

4. Process with the Sorbet setting.

5. Serve fresh for a unique, herb-infused dessert or freeze for later enjoyment.

Nutritional Information (per serving):
Calories: 200 | Fat: 0g | Carbohydrates: 51g | Protein: 1g

Watermelon Mint Sorbet

Prep Time: 10 minutes
Cook Time: N/A
Serving Size: 4 servings
Ingredients:

- 1 cup water

- 3/4 cup granulated sugar

- 4 cups watermelon, cubed and seeds removed

- 1/4 cup fresh mint leaves

Instructions:

1. Prepare a simple syrup by dissolving sugar in water over heat. Allow to cool.

2. Puree watermelon and mint until smooth.

3. Stir watermelon and mint puree into the cooled syrup.

4. Freeze in the Ninja Creami pint container for 24 hours.

5. Use the Sorbet setting to process.

6. Serve immediately for a refreshing, minty treat or store in the freezer.

Nutritional Information (per serving):
Calories: 190 | Fat: 0g | Carbohydrates: 49g | Protein: 1g

Chocolate Sorbet

Prep Time: 10 minutes
Cook Time: N/A
Serving Size: 4 servings
Ingredients:

- 1 1/2 cups water

- 1 cup granulated sugar

- 3/4 cup unsweetened cocoa powder

- 1/2 teaspoon vanilla extract

Instructions:

1. Make a simple syrup with water and sugar, then whisk in cocoa powder until smooth. Add vanilla extract.

2. Cool the mixture completely.

3. Transfer to the Ninja Creami pint container and freeze for 24 hours.

4. Process using the Sorbet setting.

5. Enjoy this rich, chocolatey sorbet immediately or freeze for later.

Nutritional Information (per serving):
Calories: 220 | Fat: 1g | Carbohydrates: 56g | Protein: 2g

Pineapple Coconut Sorbet

Prep Time: 15 minutes
Cook Time: N/A
Serving Size: 4 servings
Ingredients:

- 1 cup pineapple juice

- 3/4 cup granulated sugar

- 2 cups fresh pineapple, chopped

- 1/2 cup coconut milk

Instructions:

1. In a saucepan, dissolve sugar in pineapple juice over medium heat. Allow to cool.

2. Blend the cooled syrup with fresh pineapple and coconut milk until smooth.

3. Freeze the mixture in the Ninja Creami pint container for 24 hours.

4. Process with the Sorbet setting.

5. Serve your tropical sorbet immediately or freeze for a later indulgence.

Nutritional Information (per serving):
Calories: 230 | Fat: 5g | Carbohydrates: 48g | Protein: 1g

Strawberry Sorbet

Prep Time: 10 minutes
Cook Time: N/A
Serving Size: 4 servings
Ingredients:

- 1 cup water

- 3/4 cup granulated sugar

- 3 cups fresh strawberries, hulled

Instructions:

1. Make a simple syrup by heating sugar and water until the sugar dissolves. Cool it down.

2. Puree strawberries and mix with the cooled syrup.

3. Freeze in the Ninja Creami pint container for 24 hours.

4. Process using the Sorbet setting.

5. Serve the vibrant strawberry sorbet immediately or keep it in the freezer.

Nutritional Information (per serving):
Calories: 190 | Fat: 0g | Carbohydrates: 48g | Protein: 1g

Blueberry Lavender Sorbet

Prep Time: 15 minutes
Cook Time: N/A
Serving Size: 4 servings
Ingredients:

- 1 cup water

- 3/4 cup granulated sugar

- 1 tablespoon dried lavender flowers

- 3 cups fresh blueberries

Instructions:

1. Combine water, sugar, and lavender in a saucepan. Bring to a simmer, then cool and strain.

2. Blend the syrup with blueberries until smooth.

3. Pour into the Ninja Creami pint container and freeze for 24 hours.

4. Process with the Sorbet setting.

5. Enjoy the floral and fruity sorbet immediately, or freeze for later use.

Nutritional Information (per serving):
Calories: 200 | Fat: 0g | Carbohydrates: 51g | Protein: 1g

Kiwi Sorbet

Prep Time: 10 minutes
Cook Time: N/A
Serving Size: 4 servings
Ingredients:

- 1 cup water

- 3/4 cup granulated sugar

- 4 cups kiwi, peeled and chopped

Instructions:

1. Dissolve sugar in water over heat to make a simple syrup. Let it cool.

2. Puree kiwi and mix with the cooled syrup.

3. Freeze in the Ninja Creami pint container for 24 hours.

4. Use the Sorbet setting to process.

5. Serve this vibrant, tangy sorbet immediately or store in the freezer.

Nutritional Information (per serving):
Calories: 200 | Fat: 0.5g | Carbohydrates: 50g | Protein: 2g

Tropical Paradise Smoothie Bowl

Prep Time: 10 minutes
Cook Time: N/A
Serving Size: 2 servings
Ingredients:

- 1 frozen banana

- 1/2 cup frozen mango chunks

- 1/2 cup frozen pineapple chunks

- 1/2 cup coconut milk

- Toppings: Sliced kiwi, coconut flakes, chia seeds

Instructions:

1. Combine the banana, mango, pineapple, and coconut milk in the Ninja Creami pint container. Freeze for 24 hours.

2. Use the Smoothie Bowl setting to process until smooth.

3. Divide between two bowls and top with sliced kiwi, coconut flakes, and chia seeds.

Nutritional Information (per serving):
Calories: 250 | Fat: 12g | Carbohydrates: 36g | Protein: 3g

Berry Bliss Smoothie Bowl

Prep Time: 10 minutes
Cook Time: N/A
Serving Size: 2 servings
Ingredients:

- 1 cup frozen mixed berries (strawberries, blueberries, raspberries)

- 1 frozen banana

- 1/2 cup Greek yogurt

- Toppings: Granola, fresh berries, honey drizzle

Instructions:

1. Add the mixed berries, banana, and Greek yogurt to the Ninja Creami pint container. Freeze for 24 hours.

2. Process using the Smoothie Bowl setting until creamy.

3. Serve in bowls, topped with granola, fresh berries, and a honey drizzle.

Nutritional Information (per serving):
Calories: 220 | Fat: 2g | Carbohydrates: 46g | Protein: 8g

Green Goddess Smoothie Bowl

Prep Time: 10 minutes
Cook Time: N/A
Serving Size: 2 servings
Ingredients:

- 1 frozen banana

- 1/2 cup frozen pineapple chunks

- 1 cup spinach

- 1/2 avocado

- 1/2 cup almond milk

- Toppings: Sliced banana, hemp seeds, sliced almonds

Instructions:

1. Blend the banana, pineapple, spinach, avocado, and almond milk in the Ninja Creami pint container. Freeze for 24 hours.

2. Use the Smoothie Bowl setting to achieve a smooth consistency.

3. Top with banana slices, hemp seeds, and sliced almonds before serving.

Nutritional Information (per serving):
Calories: 230 | Fat: 11g | Carbohydrates: 31g | Protein: 5g

Peanut Butter Cup Smoothie Bowl

Prep Time: 10 minutes
Cook Time: N/A
Serving Size: 2 servings
Ingredients:

- 2 frozen bananas

- 2 tablespoons peanut butter

- 1 tablespoon cocoa powder

- 1/2 cup almond milk

- Toppings: Chopped peanuts, chocolate chips, banana slices

Instructions:

1. Combine bananas, peanut butter, cocoa powder, and almond milk in the Ninja Creami pint container. Freeze for 24 hours.

2. Process with the Smoothie Bowl setting until creamy.

3. Garnish with peanuts, chocolate chips, and banana slices.

Nutritional Information (per serving):
Calories: 340 | Fat: 18g | Carbohydrates: 42g | Protein: 10g

Acai Energy Bowl

Prep Time: 10 minutes
Cook Time: N/A
Serving Size: 2 servings
Ingredients:

- 1 frozen banana

- 1/2 cup frozen blueberries

- 1 packet frozen acai berry puree

- 1/2 cup apple juice

- Toppings: Granola, sliced strawberries, sliced banana

Instructions:

1. Mix banana, blueberries, acai puree, and apple juice in the Ninja Creami pint container. Freeze for 24 hours.

2. Use the Smoothie Bowl setting for a smooth texture.

3. Add granola, strawberries, and banana slices on top before serving.

Nutritional Information (per serving):
Calories: 210 | Fat: 5g | Carbohydrates: 42g | Protein: 3g

Chocolate Avocado Smoothie Bowl

Prep Time: 10 minutes
Cook Time: N/A
Serving Size: 2 servings
Ingredients:

- 1 frozen banana

- 1/2 avocado

- 2 tablespoons cocoa powder

- 1/2 cup coconut milk

- Toppings: Cocoa nibs, sliced almonds, coconut flakes

Instructions:

1. Blend banana, avocado, cocoa powder, and coconut milk in the Ninja Creami pint container. Freeze for 24 hours.

2. Process using the Smoothie Bowl setting until creamy.

3. Decorate with cocoa nibs, almonds, and coconut flakes.

Nutritional Information (per serving):
Calories: 280 | Fat: 19g | Carbohydrates: 30g | Protein: 4g

Sunrise Mango Smoothie Bowl

Prep Time: 10 minutes
Cook Time: N/A
Serving Size: 2 servings
Ingredients:

- 1 cup frozen mango chunks

- 1/2 frozen banana

- 1/2 cup orange juice

- 1/2 cup Greek yogurt

- Toppings: Sliced kiwi, mango chunks, chia seeds

Instructions:

1. Combine mango, banana, orange juice, and Greek yogurt in the Ninja Creami pint container. Freeze for 24 hours.

2. Process with the Smoothie Bowl setting until smooth.

3. Serve with kiwi slices, mango chunks, and a sprinkle of chia seeds.

Nutritional Information (per serving):
Calories: 220 | Fat: 1g | Carbohydrates: 48g | Protein: 8g

Super Berry Antioxidant Bowl

Prep Time: 10 minutes
Cook Time: N/A
Serving Size: 2 servings
Ingredients:

- 1 cup frozen mixed berries

- 1/2 frozen banana

- 1/2 cup pomegranate juice

- 1/2 cup Greek yogurt

- Toppings: Fresh berries, flax seeds, granola

Instructions:

1. Mix the berries, banana, pomegranate juice, and Greek yogurt in the Ninja Creami pint container. Freeze for 24 hours.

2. Use the Smoothie Bowl setting to achieve a creamy consistency.

3. Top with berries, flax seeds, and granola before serving.

Nutritional Information (per serving):
Calories: 210 | Fat: 2g | Carbohydrates: 44g | Protein: 8g

Matcha Green Tea Smoothie Bowl

Prep Time: 10 minutes
Cook Time: N/A
Serving Size: 2 servings
Ingredients:

- 1 frozen banana

- 1 teaspoon matcha green tea powder

- 1/2 cup spinach

- 1/2 cup coconut milk

- Toppings: Sliced banana, coconut flakes, chia seeds

Instructions:

1. Blend banana, matcha powder, spinach, and coconut milk in the Ninja Creami pint container. Freeze for 24 hours.

2. Process with the Smoothie Bowl setting until smooth.

3. Garnish with banana slices, coconut flakes, and chia seeds.

Nutritional Information (per serving):
Calories: 180 | Fat: 11g | Carbohydrates: 20g | Protein: 3g

Pumpkin Pie Smoothie Bowl

Prep Time: 10 minutes
Cook Time: N/A
Serving Size: 2 servings
Ingredients:

- 1 frozen banana

- 1/2 cup pumpkin puree

- 1 teaspoon pumpkin pie spice

- 1/2 cup almond milk

- Toppings: Granola, pecans, a drizzle of maple syrup

Instructions:

1. Combine banana, pumpkin puree, pumpkin pie spice, and almond milk in the Ninja Creami pint container. Freeze for 24 hours.

2. Use the Smoothie Bowl setting to process until creamy.

3. Top with granola, pecans, and maple syrup before serving.

Nutritional Information (per serving):
Calories: 190 | Fat: 5g | Carbohydrates: 35g | Protein: 4g

Blueberry Flaxseed Smoothie Bowl

Prep Time: 10 minutes
Cook Time: N/A
Serving Size: 2 servings
Ingredients:

- 1 cup frozen blueberries

- 1 frozen banana

- 1 tablespoon ground flaxseed

- 1/2 cup almond milk

- Toppings: Sliced almonds, blueberries, a sprinkle of ground flaxseed

Instructions:

1. Blend blueberries, banana, ground flaxseed, and almond milk in the Ninja Creami pint container. Freeze for 24 hours.

2. Process using the Smoothie Bowl setting until smooth.

3. Garnish with almonds, extra blueberries, and a sprinkle of flaxseed.

Nutritional Information (per serving):

Calories: 150 | Fat: 3g | Carbohydrates: 30g | Protein: 3g

Peachy Keen Smoothie Bowl

Prep Time: 10 minutes
Cook Time: N/A
Serving Size: 2 servings
Ingredients:

- 1 cup frozen peaches
- 1/2 frozen banana
- 1/2 cup Greek yogurt
- 1/2 cup orange juice
- Toppings: Sliced peaches, granola, honey drizzle

Instructions:

1. Combine peaches, banana, Greek yogurt, and orange juice in the Ninja Creami pint container. Freeze for 24 hours.

2. Process with the Smoothie Bowl setting until creamy.

3. Top with peach slices, granola, and a drizzle of honey.

Nutritional Information (per serving):

Calories: 190 | Fat: 1g | Carbohydrates: 42g | Protein: 6g

Cacao Power Smoothie Bowl

Prep Time: 10 minutes
Cook Time: N/A
Serving Size: 2 servings
Ingredients:

- 1 frozen banana

- 2 tablespoons raw cacao powder

- 1/2 avocado

- 1/2 cup almond milk

- Toppings: Cacao nibs, banana slices, chia seeds

Instructions:

1. Blend banana, cacao powder, avocado, and almond milk in the Ninja Creami pint container. Freeze for 24 hours.

2. Use the Smoothie Bowl setting to process until smooth.

3. Sprinkle with cacao nibs, banana slices, and chia seeds.

Nutritional Information (per serving):
Calories: 220 | Fat: 12g | Carbohydrates: 29g | Protein: 4g

Zesty Lime and Avocado Smoothie Bowl

Prep Time: 10 minutes
Cook Time: N/A
Serving Size: 2 servings
Ingredients:

- 1 frozen banana

- 1/2 ripe avocado

- Juice of 1 lime

- 1/2 cup coconut water

- Toppings: Sliced kiwi, coconut flakes, lime zest

Instructions:

1. Mix banana, avocado, lime juice, and coconut water in the Ninja Creami pint container. Freeze for 24 hours.

2. Process with the Smoothie Bowl setting until creamy.

3. Serve topped with kiwi slices, coconut flakes, and lime zest.

Nutritional Information (per serving):
Calories: 180 | Fat: 8g | Carbohydrates: 28g | Protein: 2g

Raspberry Beet Smoothie Bowl

Prep Time: 10 minutes
Cook Time: N/A
Serving Size: 2 servings
Ingredients:

- 1 cup frozen raspberries

- 1/2 cup cooked beet, peeled and diced

- 1/2 frozen banana

- 1/2 cup almond milk

- Toppings: Fresh raspberries, chia seeds, mint leaves

Instructions:

1. Combine raspberries, beet, banana, and almond milk in the Ninja Creami pint container. Freeze for 24 hours.

2. Use the Smoothie Bowl setting to achieve a smooth texture.

3. Decorate with raspberries, chia seeds, and mint before serving.

Nutritional Information (per serving):
Calories: 140 | Fat: 2g | Carbohydrates: 30g | Protein: 3g

Spirulina Superfood Bowl

Prep Time: 10 minutes
Cook Time: N/A
Serving Size: 2 servings
Ingredients:

- 1 frozen banana

- 1 teaspoon spirulina powder

- 1/2 cup frozen pineapple chunks

- 1/2 cup coconut water

- Toppings: Sliced banana, kiwi, hemp seeds

Instructions:

1. Blend banana, spirulina, pineapple, and coconut water in the Ninja Creami pint container. Freeze for 24 hours.

2. Process using the Smoothie Bowl setting until creamy.

3. Add toppings of banana, kiwi, and hemp seeds.

Nutritional Information (per serving):
Calories: 160 | Fat: 1g | Carbohydrates: 37g | Protein: 3g

Tropical Mango Smoothie Bowl

Prep Time: 10 minutes
Cook Time: N/A
Serving Size: 2 servings
Ingredients:

- 1 cup frozen mango chunks

- 1/2 frozen banana

- 1/2 cup Greek yogurt

- 1/2 cup coconut milk

- Toppings: Mango slices, coconut flakes, a drizzle of honey

Instructions:

1. Mix mango, banana, Greek yogurt, and coconut milk in the Ninja Creami pint container. Freeze for 24 hours.

2. Process with the Smoothie Bowl setting until smooth.

3. Serve with mango slices, coconut flakes, and honey.

Nutritional Information (per serving):
Calories: 210 | Fat: 5g | Carbohydrates: 38g | Protein: 6g

Green Tea Almond Smoothie Bowl
Prep Time: 10 minutes
Cook Time: N/A
Serving Size: 2 servings
Ingredients:

- 1 frozen banana

- 1 teaspoon matcha green tea powder

- 1/2 cup frozen spinach

- 1/2 cup almond milk

- Toppings: Sliced almonds, banana slices, a drizzle of almond butter

Instructions:

1. Combine banana, matcha powder, spinach, and almond milk in the Ninja Creami pint container. Freeze for 24 hours.

2. Use the Smoothie Bowl setting to process until creamy.

3. Top with almond slices, extra banana, and almond butter.

Nutritional Information (per serving):
Calories: 180 | Fat: 8g | Carbohydrates: 25g | Protein: 4g

Berry Antioxidant Smoothie Bowl

Prep Time: 10 minutes
Cook Time: N/A
Serving Size: 2 servings
Ingredients:

- 1 cup frozen mixed berries (strawberries, blueberries, raspberries)

- 1/2 frozen banana

- 1/2 cup almond milk

- 1 tablespoon flaxseed oil

- Toppings: Fresh berries, a sprinkle of granola, a drizzle of honey

Instructions:

1. Blend mixed berries, banana, almond milk, and flaxseed oil in the Ninja Creami pint container. Freeze for 24 hours.

2. Process with the Smoothie Bowl setting until smooth.

3. Garnish with fresh berries, granola, and honey.

Nutritional Information (per serving):
Calories: 160 | Fat: 7g | Carbohydrates: 23g | Protein: 2g

Chocolate Peanut Butter Smoothie Bowl

Prep Time: 10 minutes
Cook Time: N/A
Serving Size: 2 servings
Ingredients:

- 1 frozen banana

- 2 tablespoons peanut butter

- 1 tablespoon cocoa powder

- 1/2 cup almond milk

- Toppings: Banana slices, a sprinkle of cocoa powder, peanut butter drizzle

Instructions:

1. Mix banana, peanut butter, cocoa powder, and almond milk in the Ninja Creami pint container. Freeze for 24 hours.

2. Use the Smoothie Bowl setting to achieve a creamy texture.

3. Serve topped with banana slices, extra cocoa, and a drizzle of peanut butter.

Nutritional Information (per serving):

Calories: 280 | Fat: 16g | Carbohydrates: 30g | Protein: 8g

Classic Vanilla Milkshake

Prep Time: 5 minutes
Cook Time: N/A
Serving Size: 2 servings
Ingredients:

- 1 cup vanilla ice cream

- 1/2 cup whole milk

- 1 teaspoon vanilla extract

Instructions:

1. Combine vanilla ice cream, whole milk, and vanilla extract in the Ninja Creami pint container.

2. Select the Milkshake function and process until smooth.

3. Serve immediately.

Nutritional Information (per serving):
Calories: 210 | Fat: 12g | Carbohydrates: 22g | Protein: 4g

Chocolate Peanut Butter Milkshake

Prep Time: 5 minutes
Cook Time: N/A
Serving Size: 2 servings
Ingredients:

- 1 cup chocolate ice cream

- 1/2 cup whole milk

- 2 tablespoons peanut butter

Instructions:

1. Add chocolate ice cream, whole milk, and peanut butter to the Ninja Creami pint container.

2. Use the Milkshake setting to blend until creamy.

3. Enjoy immediately.

Nutritional Information (per serving):
Calories: 330 | Fat: 21g | Carbohydrates: 29g | Protein: 9g

Strawberry Cheesecake Milkshake

Prep Time: 5 minutes
Cook Time: N/A
Serving Size: 2 servings
Ingredients:

- 1 cup strawberry ice cream
- 1/2 cup whole milk
- 1/4 cup cheesecake pieces
- 1 tablespoon strawberry syrup

Instructions:

1. Blend strawberry ice cream, whole milk, cheesecake pieces, and strawberry syrup in the Ninja Creami pint container.

2. Select the Milkshake function and process until smooth.

3. Pour into glasses and serve immediately.

Nutritional Information (per serving):
Calories: 320 | Fat: 18g | Carbohydrates: 34g | Protein: 6g

Mint Chocolate Chip Milkshake

Prep Time: 5 minutes
Cook Time: N/A
Serving Size: 2 servings
Ingredients:

- 1 cup mint chocolate chip ice cream

- 1/2 cup whole milk

- Chocolate chips for garnish

Instructions:

1. Combine mint chocolate chip ice cream and whole milk in the Ninja Creami pint container.

2. Use the Milkshake setting to blend until creamy.

3. Garnish with chocolate chips and serve.

Nutritional Information (per serving):
Calories: 280 | Fat: 15g | Carbohydrates: 33g | Protein: 5g

Salted Caramel Pretzel Milkshake

Prep Time: 5 minutes
Cook Time: N/A
Serving Size: 2 servings
Ingredients:

- 1 cup caramel ice cream

- 1/2 cup whole milk

- 1/4 cup crushed pretzels

- 1 tablespoon salted caramel sauce

Instructions:

1. Mix caramel ice cream, whole milk, crushed pretzels, and salted caramel sauce in the Ninja Creami pint container.

2. Select the Milkshake function and blend until smooth.

3. Drizzle with extra caramel sauce and sprinkle with pretzel pieces before serving.

Nutritional Information (per serving):
Calories: 310 | Fat: 14g | Carbohydrates: 42g | Protein: 7g

Cookies and Cream Milkshake

Prep Time: 5 minutes
Cook Time: N/A
Serving Size: 2 servings
Ingredients:

- 1 cup cookies and cream ice cream
- 1/2 cup whole milk
- 2 tablespoons crushed cookies

Instructions:

1. Add cookies and cream ice cream, whole milk, and crushed cookies to the Ninja Creami pint container.
2. Use the Milkshake setting to process until creamy.
3. Top with additional crushed cookies and serve immediately.

Nutritional Information (per serving):
Calories: 320 | Fat: 17g | Carbohydrates: 36g | Protein: 5g

Banana Nutella Milkshake

Prep Time: 5 minutes
Cook Time: N/A
Serving Size: 2 servings
Ingredients:

- 1 cup vanilla ice cream
- 1/2 cup whole milk
- 1 ripe banana

- 2 tablespoons Nutella

Instructions:

1. Combine vanilla ice cream, whole milk, banana, and Nutella in the Ninja Creami pint container.

2. Select the Milkshake function and blend until smooth.

3. Serve topped with a swirl of Nutella.

Nutritional Information (per serving):
Calories: 350 | Fat: 16g | Carbohydrates: 46g | Protein: 6g

Blueberry Muffin Milkshake
Prep Time: 5 minutes
Cook Time: N/A
Serving Size: 2 servings
Ingredients:

- 1 cup blueberry ice cream
- 1/2 cup whole milk
- 1/4 cup crumbled blueberry muffin

Instructions:

1. Blend blueberry ice cream, whole milk, and crumbled blueberry muffin in the Ninja Creami pint container.

2. Process using the Milkshake setting until creamy.

3. Serve immediately, garnished with extra muffin crumbles.

Nutritional Information (per serving):
Calories: 310 | Fat: 14g | Carbohydrates: 40g | Protein: 5g

Peach Cobbler Milkshake

Prep Time: 5 minutes
Cook Time: N/A
Serving Size: 2 servings
Ingredients:

- 1 cup peach ice cream
- 1/2 cup whole milk
- 1/4 cup peach pieces
- 1/4 cup crumbled cobbler topping

Instructions:

1. Combine peach ice cream, whole milk, peach pieces, and cobbler topping in the Ninja Creami pint container.

2. Use the Milkshake function to blend until smooth.

3. Serve garnished with extra peach pieces and cobbler crumbles.

Nutritional Information (per serving):
Calories: 290 | Fat: 14g | Carbohydrates: 36g | Protein: 5g

Mocha Java Milkshake

Prep Time: 5 minutes
Cook Time: N/A
Serving Size: 2 servings
Ingredients:

- 1 cup coffee ice cream
- 1/2 cup whole milk
- 1 tablespoon chocolate syrup
- 1 teaspoon instant coffee granules

Instructions:

1. Mix coffee ice cream, whole milk, chocolate syrup, and instant coffee granules in the Ninja Creami pint container.

2. Select the Milkshake setting and process until creamy.

3. Serve immediately, optionally garnished with whipped cream and a drizzle of chocolate syrup.

Nutritional Information (per serving):
Calories: 260 | Fat: 14g | Carbohydrates: 29g | Protein: 5g

Pumpkin Spice Milkshake

Prep Time: 5 minutes
Cook Time: N/A
Serving Size: 2 servings
Ingredients:

- 1 cup pumpkin spice ice cream

- 1/2 cup whole milk

- 1/4 teaspoon pumpkin pie spice

- Whipped cream, for garnish

- Cinnamon stick, for garnish

Instructions:

1. Combine pumpkin spice ice cream, whole milk, and pumpkin pie spice in the Ninja Creami pint container.

2. Use the Milkshake function to blend until smooth.

3. Serve immediately, topped with whipped cream and a cinnamon stick.

Nutritional Information (per serving):
Calories: 250 | Fat: 12g | Carbohydrates: 30g | Protein: 4g

Raspberry White Chocolate Milkshake

Prep Time: 5 minutes
Cook Time: N/A
Serving Size: 2 servings
Ingredients:

- 1 cup vanilla ice cream

- 1/2 cup whole milk

- 1/2 cup fresh raspberries

- 2 tablespoons white chocolate chips

Instructions:

1. Add vanilla ice cream, whole milk, raspberries, and white chocolate chips to the Ninja Creami pint container.

2. Process using the Milkshake function until creamy.

3. Serve immediately, garnished with extra raspberries and white chocolate chips.

Nutritional Information (per serving):
Calories: 320 | Fat: 18g | Carbohydrates: 36g | Protein: 5g

Key Lime Pie Milkshake

Prep Time: 5 minutes
Cook Time: N/A
Serving Size: 2 servings
Ingredients:

- 1 cup lime sherbet

- 1/2 cup whole milk

- 1/4 cup crushed graham crackers

- Whipped cream, for garnish

- Lime slice, for garnish

Instructions:

1. Blend lime sherbet, whole milk, and crushed graham crackers in the Ninja Creami pint container.

2. Select the Milkshake function and process until smooth.

3. Serve immediately, topped with whipped cream and a lime slice.

Nutritional Information (per serving):
Calories: 230 | Fat: 7g | Carbohydrates: 39g | Protein: 3g

Caramel Apple Milkshake

Prep Time: 5 minutes
Cook Time: N/A
Serving Size: 2 servings
Ingredients:

- 1 cup apple cider sorbet or vanilla ice cream

- 1/2 cup whole milk

- 1/4 cup chopped apples

- 2 tablespoons caramel sauce

Instructions:

1. Combine apple cider sorbet (or vanilla ice cream), whole milk, apples, and caramel sauce in the Ninja Creami pint container.

2. Use the Milkshake setting to blend until smooth.

3. Drizzle with extra caramel sauce and serve immediately.

Nutritional Information (per serving):
Calories: 260 | Fat: 8g | Carbohydrates: 44g | Protein: 3g

S'mores Milkshake

Prep Time: 5 minutes
Cook Time: N/A
Serving Size: 2 servings
Ingredients:

- 1 cup chocolate ice cream

- 1/2 cup whole milk

- 1/4 cup crushed graham crackers

- 2 tablespoons marshmallow fluff

- Chocolate syrup, for garnish

- Mini marshmallows, for garnish

Instructions:

1. Mix chocolate ice cream, whole milk, crushed graham crackers, and marshmallow fluff in the Ninja Creami pint container.

2. Process using the Milkshake function until creamy.

3. Garnish with chocolate syrup and mini marshmallows before serving.

Nutritional Information (per serving):

Calories: 350 | Fat: 16g | Carbohydrates: 47g | Protein: 5g

Maple Walnut Milkshake

Prep Time: 5 minutes
Cook Time: N/A
Serving Size: 2 servings
Ingredients:

- 1 cup walnut ice cream

- 1/2 cup whole milk

- 2 tablespoons maple syrup

- Chopped walnuts, for garnish

Instructions:

1. Combine walnut ice cream, whole milk, and maple syrup in the Ninja Creami pint container.

2. Select the Milkshake function and blend until smooth.

3. Top with chopped walnuts and serve immediately.

Nutritional Information (per serving):
Calories: 310 | Fat: 18g | Carbohydrates: 33g | Protein: 6g

17. Birthday Cake Milkshake

Prep Time: 5 minutes
Cook Time: N/A
Serving Size: 2 servings
Ingredients:

- 1 cup cake batter ice cream

- 1/2 cup whole milk

- 1/4 cup sprinkles

- Whipped cream, for garnish

- More sprinkles, for garnish

Instructions:

1. Blend cake batter ice cream, whole milk, and sprinkles in the Ninja Creami pint container.

2. Use the Milkshake setting to process until creamy.

3. Serve topped with whipped cream and more sprinkles.

Nutritional Information (per serving):
Calories: 280 | Fat: 14g | Carbohydrates: 34g | Protein: 5g

Chocolate Peanut Butter Milkshake

Prep Time: 5 minutes
Cook Time: N/A
Serving Size: 2 servings
Ingredients:

- 1 cup chocolate ice cream

- 1/2 cup whole milk

- 2 tablespoons peanut butter

- Chocolate chips, for garnish

- Peanut butter cup, for garnish

Instructions:

1. Mix chocolate ice cream, whole milk, and peanut butter in the Ninja Creami pint container.

2. Select the Milkshake setting and process until smooth.

3. Garnish with chocolate chips and a peanut butter cup before serving.

Nutritional Information (per serving):
Calories: 370 | Fat: 22g | Carbohydrates: 36g | Protein: 10g

Strawberry Cheesecake Milkshake

Prep Time: 5 minutes
Cook Time: N/A
Serving Size: 2 servings
Ingredients:

- 1 cup strawberry ice cream

- 1/2 cup whole milk

- 1/4 cup cheesecake pieces

- 1/4 cup fresh strawberries, for garnish

- Graham cracker crumbs, for garnish

Instructions:

1. Combine strawberry ice cream, whole milk, and cheesecake pieces in the Ninja Creami pint container.

2. Use the Milkshake function to blend until creamy.

3. Garnish with fresh strawberries and graham cracker crumbs before serving.

Nutritional Information (per serving):
Calories: 320 | Fat: 18g | Carbohydrates: 34g | Protein: 6g

Mint Chocolate Chip Milkshake

Prep Time: 5 minutes
Cook Time: N/A
Serving Size: 2 servings
Ingredients:

- 1 cup mint chocolate chip ice cream

- 1/2 cup whole milk

- Chocolate chips, for garnish

- Mint leaves, for garnish

Instructions:

1. Blend mint chocolate chip ice cream and whole milk in the Ninja Creami pint container.

2. Process using the Milkshake setting until smooth.

3. Serve garnished with chocolate chips and mint leaves.

Nutritional Information (per serving):
Calories: 290 | Fat: 15g | Carbohydrates: 33g | Protein: 5g

Conclusion

Beginning the path of preparing frozen delicacies with your Ninja Creami provides a wonderful and imaginative culinary experience, as demonstrated in this beginner cookbook. You've unlocked the potential to transform your kitchen into a gourmet ice cream parlor by learning the ins and outs of your Ninja Creami, mastering basic techniques, and experimenting with a wide range of recipes including lite ice creams, indulgent mix-ins, classic flavors, gelatos, sorbets, smoothie bowls, and milkshakes.

Each recipe has been meticulously developed not only to inspire, but also to ensure that you get great results every time, regardless of your skill level. The nutritional information supplied with each dish promotes mindful indulgence, allowing you to enjoy these frozen treats while remaining conscious of your dietary choices.

As you continue to explore your Ninja Creami's capabilities, keep in mind that cooking and creating is all about personalizing and having fun. Don't be afraid to experiment with flavors, textures, and ingredients. Because of the Ninja Creami's versatility, the options are practically limitless, encouraging you to experiment and possibly even create your own trademark frozen delicacy.

We hope this cookbook serves as a starting point for your Ninja Creami journey, inspiring delight and creativity with each scoop. May your days be filled with the sweet enjoyment of homemade frozen treats, bringing joy to the faces of friends and family. Remember that the best ingredient in any recipe is the love and excitement you bring to it. Have fun crafting!

Printed in Great Britain
by Amazon

41651748R00046